POWER HOUSE

Phillip Guy-Bromley as Farfarello in **The Love for Three Oranges** 1990

POWER HOUSE
The English National Opera Experience

PETER JONAS, MARK ELDER and DAVID POUNTNEY
Introduction by THE EARL OF HAREWOOD
Photographs by BILL RAFFERTY

Additional photographs by
Clive Barda, Jim Caldwell, Tim Flach,
Donald Southern and Reg Wilson

Compiled and edited by Nicholas John

Cathryn Pope as
Mélisande and
Willard White as
Golaud
**Pelléas and
Mélisande**
Debussy/
Maeterlinck
conductor: Mark
Elder, *producer:*
David Pountney,
designer: Marie-
Jeanne Lecca,
lighting: Richard
Riddell, *translator:*
Hugh Macdonald
1990

LIME
TREE

First published in Great Britain 1992
by Lime Tree
an imprint of Reed Consumer Books Ltd
Michelin House, 81 Fulham Road, London sw3 6rb
and Auckland, Melbourne, Singapore and Toronto

Introduction copyright © 1992 The Earl of Harewood
A Polemic © 1992 Peter Jonas, Mark Elder, David Pountney
Company history copyright © 1992 Nicholas John

The authors have asserted their moral rights

A CIP catalogue record for this book
is available from the British Library
ISBN 0 413 45631 5

Photoset by Rowland Phototypesetting Limited
Bury St Edmunds, Suffolk
Printed and bound in Great Britain
by BPCC Hazells Ltd

The London
Coliseum (photo:
Tim Flach)

Introduction

If you ask what is the aim of an opera company, the straight answer must be 'to perform opera to as high a standard as lies within the company's possibilities – and then to raise standards a bit higher'. All other considerations – of place, specialization, casting, tradition and so on – are secondary, and if they are not found so, the person answering the question should not be in any position of operatic responsibility. On the other hand, if you ask how this aim is to be accomplished, there are almost as many answers as there are opera companies. This book chronicles one.

Early in my opera-loving life, senior opera-goers used sagely to point to pre-war Glyndebourne as a golden age and ascribe the success first and foremost to the partnership of Fritz Busch and Carl Ebert, conductor and producer, who were jointly responsible for every one of Glyndebourne's early productions. Their work was held aloft as a kind of talisman, something post-war managers (to bring it down from the frequently sublime to the nearly ridiculous, they would imply) should aim for if they would only focus their sights on the ideal as opposed to the mundane.

When in 1979 ENO appointed Mark Elder as Music Director, he said at the outset that he believed he would do his best work with David Pountney (they had worked together at Cambridge and had at the Coliseum already collaborated on *Toussaint*). The way ahead seemed clear. A positive partnership such as was being proposed could conceivably add up to more than the sum of its two components and powerfully affect the company's style. Of course, there was a risk. There is a big difference between a company's style and a 'company style', and the latter, even combined with a vision for the future, presupposes a certain exclusiveness. Nor probably will it involve a policy with a safety net, so that the artist's 'right to fail' (which basically means to experiment) will have from time to time to be invoked. But if the mixture is right the benefits will far outweigh the disadvantages, and the decade following David Pountney's appointment proved Mark Elder right. Some of the boldest experiments were nothing short of a revelation – I would subjectively point to *Rusalka*, *Osud*, *Lady Macbeth of Mtsensk* and *Hansel and Gretel* as belonging to that category, but other opera-goers will make other choices. What is unquestionable is that the joint influence of Elder and Pountney affected productions in which only one (or perhaps neither) was concerned but which explored certain works as they had rarely been explored before.

Discussion of the achievement of Busch and Ebert did not invariably involve mention of the name of Rudolf Bing who was Glyndebourne's manager, but it would be quite wrong not to bring Peter Jonas's into stellar conjunction with those of the Music Director and Director of Productions for the entire period (1985–93) for which he has been General Director. A manager is responsible for the work of a company as a whole, and, while it might theoretically be possible for individual productions to flourish in spite of him, a company style could hardly develop without his enthusiasm. I hope foundations were already in place before Peter Jonas arrived, but what was built up after 1985 is without a doubt considerably his achievement.

This book celebrates the work first of all of Mark Elder, who was in position longest of the three and who set the musical standards without which an opera company is trading under false pretences. Then, it highlights the penetrating enthusiasm of David Pountney and what he and his team of producer/directors offered the public within a given period. Finally, it suggests the operatic aesthetic of Peter Jonas, whose love of opera had been hidden for years under a symphonic bushel in Chicago but who proved a worthy follower in line from the great Lilian Baylis, without whom none of it might have happened. And I think it suggests the triumvirate knew what the aim of an opera company should be.

Lord Harewood

A Polemic

ENO has been called provocative, challenging, irreverent, iconoclastic, cheeky, populist, vulgar, outrageous, wilful, radical. Yet this book is a salute to tradition. Not, of course, the tradition that opera is a stuffy, grandiose art-form pandering to and reassuring the Establishment, but the tradition of Lilian Baylis, whose idealism led to the founding of opera, theatre and ballet companies in unfashionable parts of London. She believed that the 'rest' deserved the best too, and in order to achieve this her idealism was tempered by a robust practicality. When a singer asked her for more money, she would say: 'Let's ask God, shall we?', close her eyes for a moment, and then reply sadly: 'God says "No", I'm afraid.' God frequently said 'No' during the 1980s.

For us, survival through this rather unpleasant decade was an exciting obstacle race – fun to win but dangerous to lose. There were, and still are, plenty of philistines of left and right just waiting for a missed footing. Opera is an easy target for the idealogues of the left who decline to make a distinction between Rembrandt and rap, Keats and 'Kilroy', or Bach and a busker. Opera requires a host of formidable skills to perform and create; it is Eurocentric – indeed it is a pinnacle of Western, European culture – and it is largely created by Dead White Males. It is costly to produce and to watch, politically – gloriously – incorrect: in short, elitist. But Lilian Baylis wanted everyone to have their slice of the elitist cake. For her culture was an improving thing – a view which might now sound patronizing. Yet it is the art-form which is improved by healthy interaction with a wide non-specialist audience, while the audience is simultaneously nourished by its consumption.

From the right come the less wordy but no less lethal cavalry who would like to scythe down the entire notion of subsidized culture. If opera is elitist and expensive, that's good so long as its consumers pay for it themselves. After all, Lilian Baylis had no subsidy. This attitude is summed up by Margaret Thatcher's disgraceful remark: 'There is no such thing as society.' The economist Hayek may be correct that, since the economy is the result of infinite intricate personal decisions, no government can ever second guess the intentions behind those decisions and, therefore, the market must rule. But if so, it may be precisely because of the lonely individuality of economic and commercial life that society seeks to compensate by defining itself in culture.

Opera houses, art galleries, museums, libraries, theatres and concert halls are an expression of society's unconscious desire to share the communal experience of the enjoyment and emotional and intellectual fulfilment they offer. The architecture of these buildings often reflects the fact that society feels itself ennobled in their possession. In the West End of London the commercial and the subsidized exist side by side and interact and relate to one another, and this, if anything, clarifies their respective roles. Art has the duty to entertain because, if it does not, it speaks only to itself, which is ultimately a decadent and futile process. But in its examination of

Toussaint David Blake/Anthony Ward: *conductor:* Mark Elder, *producer:* David Pountney, *designer:* Maria Bjørnson, *lighting:* Nick Chelton 1977 (photo: Reg Wilson)

9

the 'inner', the hidden, the potential, it has a duty to disturb and to question. Just as a wise king always has a critic (and a fool) at his court, so a healthy society encourages art that goes beyond the satisfaction of its immediate need to be delighted to subvert and challenge the *status quo*. A society elects to relieve a portion of its artistic life from purely commercial pressures not necessarily because it expects the subsidized results to be *per se* better but both more dangerous and more widely accessible than they would otherwise be. Our emotional, intellectual and commercial lives are obviously closely related, but they give rise to very different emphases. A subsidized art-form exists to explore emotional and intellectual realities beyond the obvious, in the realm of value rather than price.

This journey of exploration is not one that every member of society will choose to make. Art is essential, but not strictly necessary. Hitherto, social elites have demonstrated their special right to lead or to dominate by establishing near-exclusive ownership of culture, bolstering their sense of solidarity in the communal enjoyment of privilege. Even the Coliseum, with its embarrassing separate entrance to the balcony – in an alley round the corner – still perpetuates this class exclusivity. But Lilian Baylis saw that adventures of the heart and the mind, whilst not necessary or desirable for everyone, should necessarily and desirably be available and accessible to everyone. An artistic event would then be not the reinforcement of social exclusivity but an opportunity to forge the bonds of a shared experience.

The experience of an evening at the opera is frequently a very messy affair and, often enough, laughably short of the ideal which could justify these utopian aims. But the underlying integrity of these aims must always underpin the fragility of their achievement because the integrity of culture is one of the few things, besides religion, that can sustain the notion that somewhere there is a real meaning, a real heart, to our continued, communal existence. Without it, the squalor of mean survival is surely unbearable.

The experience of opera touches at this heart in two ways. Like all theatre, it keeps alive a tenuous link with its origins in ritual and, therefore, with the essential need of any coherent society to share rituals. If we separate these rituals crudely into the sacred and the profane, we can say that in the one society examines its relationship with God, in the other its relationship with itself. Whatever we may feel about the various merits of different religious structures, there can surely be no question that society itself is weakened by the fact that it scarcely continues to share any element of sacred ritual. This perhaps places a burden on the profane ritual of theatre that it is scarcely able to fulfil. We can see the expression of this uneasy sense of deficiency in the continual attempts by the language of the media to find a moral content in the quasi-theatrical rituals of sport. Opera occupies a unique position in profane ritual because the relationship between the abstract and emotional world of music and the more concrete, social world of text constantly gives opera a connection to the deeper mysteries of the sacred. That is how a medium which is, on one level, so vulgar and crude is, on another, so profound. There are many very trivial reasons for the eruption in opera's popularity over the last decade

Alan Woodrow as Herod and Kristine Ciesinski as Salome (1991 revival)
Salome R. Strauss/ Lachmann: *conductor:* Mark Elder, *producer:* Joachim Herz, *designer:* Rudolf Heinrich, *lighting:* Rudolf Heinrich, *translator:* Tom Hammond 1975

– the ad-man's discovery of opera's blend of corny emotion with glamour and spectacle, the fashionable cravings of yuppie culture snackers – but the public's obsession with opera survives through the recession and seems to show a search for an emotional experience: a sacred and profane ritual all in one. Perhaps this is not surprising after a decade of unparalleled cynical materialism.

Christopher Robson with the Shepherds and Villagers, and Anthony Rolfe Johnson as Orfeo (1992 revival)
Orfeo Monteverdi/ Striggio: *conductor:* John Eliot Gardiner, *producer:* David Freeman, *designers:* Hayden Griffin/ Peter Hartwell, *lighting:* Stephen Watson/revival by Rory Dempster, *translator:* Anne Ridler 1981

Opera is a very clumsy medium for the expression of political ideologies – its brush is too broad for all those sub-clauses and selective hatreds. Yet political *feeling*, rather than ideology, is at the heart of all great opera. Its massed forces instinctively address the unspoken areas of emotional politics that are, in the long run, more fundamental. In so doing, it also illuminates the politics of personal relations: the vital fabric of social life that exists in the silence between people – exactly that space which is filled by music. Janáček described this space precisely: 'As the person talked to me in a conventional conversation, I knew, I heard that, inside himself, the person perhaps wept.' This reveals exactly the function of music in opera: it is to give expression to that inner voice. Indeed, in opera, the world is turned inside out for it is the inner voice, the music, which dominates and 'conventional conversation' which is the background. The communal act of listening to, and becoming aware of, the 'inner voice' in each of us is a crucial social experience.

What a book of pictures cannot celebrate is the music which is the heart of the operatic experience. Opera has appeared in history in so many different forms that it has become very difficult to define, but one central requirement remains: it is a drama conveyed *through* music. A musical, by contrast, is a drama *accompanied* by music. In opera the music inseminates the drama, and the orchestra, placed strategically between audience and stage, gives depth and vitality to the dramatic interaction between audience and performers. What we *hear* is the fundamental experience of an opera, even though it affects, and is affected by, what we see. At the opera we watch with our ears and listen with our eyes. Because music can be heard and understood in such limitlessly different ways, the ability of the visual image to affect the way we listen is powerful. For instance, the very different visual worlds of Patrice Chéreau and Wieland Wagner have given us two very different aural as well as visual perspectives on Richard Wagner's operas. That is why the role of the conductor is so pivotal and goes beyond simply ensuring the best possible musical performance. The ideal opera conductor is one whose musical and theatrical sensibilities enable him or her to conduct both the production and the score, igniting their mutual potential. But this kind of integrated inspiration can only follow from the commitment of conductor and musicians to the lengthy process of preparing an opera production, as well as to a substantial run of performances. The conductor is able to transform a production by his or her musical response to it and hence his or her daily involvement is a precondition of ensemble music theatre.

A true ensemble also includes administration in all its aspects. Apparently mundane management decisions in an opera house will, way down the line, have a musical and dramatic consequence. Seat-price policy, marketing style and the colour of the carpets affect the composition of the audience, where they sit, their mood, and therefore how they watch and listen. In addition, the balance of music and drama on the stage mirrors a similar balance in society as a whole. The old soubriquet 'an irrational entertainment' is accurate in a way its author did not intend because the function of music is to represent the irrational, the instinctive and the emotional. It is perhaps because its material is so essentially volatile that it is the most precisely organized and notated of all media. Its Dionysiac tendencies are held in balance by the text which tends to the rational and Apollonian. These two opposed forces meet and are fused in the action and image of the stage. In this way an opera mirrors society's constant tidal struggle between freedom and restraint. The balance between feeling and reason, emotion and thought is the fundamental subject of opera (but not necessarily of individual operas). It is also the fundamental definition of society.

A varied and adventurous repertoire is another continuing tradition which this book celebrates. The wide-ranging lists of works performed at Sadler's Wells are a constant inspiration, though nothing can quite match the perspicacious introduction of Janáček operas, starting with *Katya Kabanova* in 1951, and continuing with *The Cunning Little Vixen*, *The Makropulos Case* and *From the House of the Dead*, by Charles Mackerras and Norman Tucker in the 1960s. Works of such genius are only rarely discovered. Indeed, the sheer difficulty of creating a successful opera dictates that there are many hundreds of interesting operas, a fair handful of masterpieces, and a tiny core of 'pops'. It is an acute problem for any company to maintain the integrity of this small group of works for which the public has such relentless enthusiasm: *The Marriage of Figaro*, *Don Giovanni*, *The Magic Flute*, *The Barber of Seville*, *La traviata*, *Rigoletto*, *Il trovatore*, *Aida*, *Carmen*, *La bohème*, *Madam Butterfly*, *Tosca*. The difficulties of casting and finance narrow the list still further. But even if it would be better to leave works like *Carmen* and *Bohème* to lie fallow for a few years, the pressure of the box office wills them back again. The pieces, of course, do not grow stale but the more often the same works are given, the more likely they are to receive stale performances. A wide repertoire is essential at the least to vary the frame around this core.

The single most influential policy decision in expanding the repertoire was Lord Harewood's scheme, which became known as the Norwest Holst series after its sponsor. This was an imaginative response to the problem of marrying limited resources of time and money to a desire to keep up a supply of new productions of non-standard works. The brief of the series was that it should contain rarely performed large-scale works by major composers. *Rienzi* (Wagner), *Mazeppa* (Tchaikovsky) and *Moses* (Rossini) were performed, and the ones that got away were Schubert's *Fierrabras* and Schumann's *Genoveva*. The productions were done on a *very* low budget, the chorus were not required to memorize their music (removing pressure from their crowded schedule) and the shows were not designed to be revived (making them much cheaper). The series was tremendously successful as a device for *instantly* enriching the repertoire but the financial constraints, combined with the knowledge that these pieces would not be revived, had the effect (which Lord Harewood had probably not envisaged) of radicalizing the production style. The very low budgets meant that anything pertaining to grandeur or spectacle had to be realized in a more or less ironic way, and the lack of the threat of a revival unleashed in Nicholas Hytner, David Alden and Keith Warner a spontaneous and irreverent bravura that made enormous impact. If we add to this *Carmen*, also done on a very low budget, these four works provided a rumbustious, iconoclastic production style quite different from the highly aesthetic and intellectual deconstruction techniques of contemporary European theatre. Many of the devices which have subsequently become known as a Coliseum cliché can be traced to this series of productions. For instance, if there is one event which defines for many the possible

Alan Woodrow as Hermann with Sarah Walker as the Countess (1986 revival)
The Queen of Spades
Tchaikovsky: *conductor:* Mark Elder, *producer:* David Pountney, *designer:* Maria Bjørnson, *lighting:* Richard Riddell, *translator:* David Lloyd-Jones 1983

excesses of so-called 'producer's opera' (*aka* Produceritis, Pountneyfication or even Aldenorrhoea) it is the 'chain-saw massacre' scene from *Mazeppa*. But this is largely a cliché of journalism rather than of the Coliseum. We certainly did not invent the notion of 'interpretative' production.

The driving influence towards 'interpretative' productions came from Germany and the reason that we think of it as a post-war phenomenon is due to the devastating gap in the development of European cultural life caused by the Nazis. One only has to read Schoenberg's comment on 'producers who look at a work only in order to see how to make it into *something quite different*' to know that the kind of thing which has produced apoplectic leaders in the *Daily Telegraph* was already current in the 1930s. In particular we can see this in the work that began at the Kroll Opera in Berlin under Klemperer, and the early careers of the two poles of German production style: Wieland Wagner (the symbolist) and Walter Felsenstein (the ultra-realist). But if the ideas were already in place in the 1930s, the practice, probably, was not. This is where Felsenstein, and his followers who worked in Britain in the 1970s, were decisively influential. Felsenstein's post-war theatre, the Komische Oper in Berlin, was probably the first to demonstrate total mastery and control over every aspect and detail of an opera performance and the meticulous application of that control towards a particular production 'concept'. It was also flawed by the fact that he never tolerated the collaboration of a first-rate conductor. His example gave opera producers a Mercedes to drive but did not tell them in which direction to drive it. Felsenstein's ruthlessly detailed and finely tuned productions were held in balance by the humanity, grace and humour that they contained; without those tempering qualities, coruscating detail can add up to a bludgeon.

Attention to detail is not, of course, quite so strong in the British temperament, so the richly talented group of directors who have worked at the Coliseum in the 1980s have happily driven the Mercedes on the wrong side of the road, put a few dents in its bodywork and filled the boot with muddy Wellingtons (not to mention suitcases, trilbies, wonky bedsteads, dark glasses and other gnomic properties). Hytner, Vick, Albery, Jones, Hollander, Alden, Miller, Freeman and Pountney represent between them a considerable diversity of style and approach, as can be seen from the work recorded in this book, but all use the machinery of 'total theatre' to reflect their own individualistic responses. This is the potential and the danger of Felsenstein's legacy: the producer has the power to take the entire opera in a particular direction, so if it is the wrong one, it is going to be a big mistake.

It is this possibility of misuse of power which has led critics to question the justification for 'interpretative' productions in principle. On the whole this debate has been conducted at a singularly feeble intellectual level, with several critics able only to arrive at the obvious conclusion that some productions are good and some bad. Yet the justification for the constant renewal, questioning and reinterpretation of opera's action and image lies at the heart of the nature of opera itself.

Arthur Davies as the
Duke and Jean
Rigby as Maddalena
Rigoletto Verdi/
Piave: *conductor:*
Mark Elder, *producer:*
Jonathan Miller,
designers: Patrick
Robertson &
Rosemary Vercoe,
lighting: Robert
Bryan, *translator:*
James Fenton 1983
(photo: Clive Barda)

Kenneth Woollam as Rienzi
Rienzi Wagner: *conductor:* Heribert
Esser, *producer:* Nicholas Hytner,
designer: David Fielding, *lighting:*
Pat Collins, *translators:* Francis
Rizzo, Robert Darling (revised by
Victor Morris) 1983 (photo: Clive
Barda)

Ethna Robinson as the Kitchen
Boy and Felicity Palmer as
Jezibaba (1991 revival)
Rusalka Dvořák/Kvapil *conductor:*
Mark Elder, *producer:* David
Pountney, *designer:* Stefanos
Lazaridis, *lighting:* Nick Chelton,
translator: Rodney Blumer 1983

Josephine Barstow as Sieglinde with the Valkyries
The Valkyrie Wagner: *conductor:* Mark Elder, *producer:* David Pountney, *designer:* Maria Bjørnson, *lighting:* Nick Chelton, *translator:* Andrew Porter 1983

Of opera's three elements, two, music and text, are relatively permanent. They live on, silently, in the score even when it is not being performed. The third element, stage action and image, is only perfunctorily described in score and libretto and its existence is therefore entirely ephemeral. Music is abstract. How often can we agree on what a piece of music is about? Yet music is precisely notated, down to the last detail. All good musical performance rests on the tension between the exactitude required simply to carry out these instructions and the creativity necessary to bring them to life. The text defines the meaning that music can only suggest but is itself much less specific about its manner of presentation. Music and text meet on the stage but the action and images that appear there have no permanence: they must be reinvented for each series of performances and on the basis of the vaguest of instructions. They are therefore the ingredients of the moment, topical, spontaneous and highly influenced by fashion. This is why the process of revival, forced on opera companies by economics, is so dangerous. It shows up very quickly the limited validity of even the best productions.

Philip Langridge as Zivny
Osud Janáček/Janáček & Bartošová: *conductor:* Mark Elder, *producer:* David Pountney, *designer:* Stefanos Lazaridis, *lighting:* Matthew Richardson, *translator:* Rodney Blumer 1984 (photo: Clive Barda)

The music and text emerge into temporary three-dimensional life in the forum of the stage which is a place of fantasy, of imagination, not of imitation. Since nothing on stage *can* be real it is quite misplaced to pretend that it is. And since what we are talking about are images and actions for music, it is clear that naturalism is out of place in opera. In any case, the common subject matter of opera defies imitation or 'accurate', 'correct' or even 'authentic' representation. What does a 'real' God wear? What does a witch's hut really look like? We may have our models, but these are all drawn from other acts of imagination. And even if we *do* know what the Count Almaviva's château looked like, we cannot fit it on the stage – so the function of the stage image is not to represent it but to evoke it imaginatively, which is a very different thing. Naturalism has its place as a brief and ephemeral theatrical fashion but even if it is appropriate in the straight theatre, which is doubtful, it is clearly inappropriate as the basis for supplying images and actions for music-theatre. If the frog on stage has to be a real frog, why doesn't the hero actually die in the last act?

Janice Cairns as Butterfly
Madam Butterfly Puccini/Giacosa & Illica: *conductor:* John Mauceri, *producer:* Graham Vick, *designer:* Stefanos Lazaridis, *lighting:* Matthew Richardson 1984

The execution
Mazeppa Tchaikovsky/Tchaikovsky & Burenin: *conductor:* Mark Elder, *producer:* David Alden, *designer:* David Fielding, *lighting:* Pat Collins, *translators:* Simon Bainbridge, Colin Pinney & Alan Reddish 1984
(photo: Clive Barda)

Dennis Wicks (He-Ancient), Helen Field (Jenifer) and Anne-Marie Owens (She-Ancient) **The Midsummer Marriage** Michael Tippett: *conductor:* Mark Elder, *producer:* David Pountney, *designers:* Stefanos Lazaridis/Sally Gardner, *lighting:* Nick Chelton 1985 (photo: Donald Southern)

This book chronicles a period in which opera in Britain distanced itself from the stylistic influence of the straight theatre and, indeed, turned the tide in the opposite direction. In the 60s and 70s theatre directors frequently moved into opera and the assumption was that they were bringing with them a more refined theatrical sense and a more sophisticated acting style than opera had hitherto exhibited. In fact, this probably represented a misunderstanding of what an appropriate acting style for opera should be. Again, the bogey is naturalism. It is ridiculous to present opera as though the performers were not actually singing. Operatic acting should flower out of, and expand upon, the inevitably larger-than-life gestures involved in the very physical act of operatic singing, not try to hide them under a pretence of drawing-room manners. This is the influence of television which, by virtue of its commercial ascendancy, has established a form of suburban naturalism as the 'approved' acting style, making it increasingly difficult to cast classical drama satisfactorily. Ironically it is through the example of opera that a more visionary, conceptual and European approach to the stage has begun to filter through into British theatre.

The view from continental Europe has also influenced the internal debate, which has continued throughout the period chronicled in this book, about what kind of company ENO should be. This debate is driven by finance on the one hand, and aesthetics on the other. Finance, or lack of it, has threatened at various moments to dictate that ENO could no longer continue to mount a year-long season or maintain a flow of new productions. The pressures of space and time in a building not designed for a nightly-changing repertoire obviously play an important part. The aesthetic question asks whether the busy, high-turnover opera house is not a thing of the past and looks enviously at the long preparation time, lavish stage facilities and large budgets available in Brussels and Amsterdam, or at Peter Stein's custom-built Schaubühne in Berlin. The debate is encapsulated in the decade's most massive operatic investment (and scandal), the Bastille. François Mitterrand's concept of a modern, populist opera house sounded like the answer to Lilian Baylis's dreams. In fact there was a characteristic and fascinating gulf between vision and practice. What the very brilliant and high-powered team assembled under Barenboim planned was a season of 'jewels' – very specialized, precisely cast, prepared and presented productions which by their nature must inevitably have been gourmet festival fare, rather than robust weekly meals for the citizens of Paris.

In the end, at ENO, the choice was finally determined by the philosophical argument – indeed by the 'Baylis' factor. This was to accept with relish that a fertile, rumbustious theatre was appropriate to a busy capital city and that an overstretched, overworked but exuberant company would provide a kind of excitement and spontaneity that is in the best tradition of British theatre. In contrast to many of our colleagues in Europe, we elected to embrace 'productivity' and it is a tribute to the willingness of the whole company to accept the pressure on working practices that that implied, that we have sustained that productivity throughout a period of considerable financial stringency. Our unions have shown a remarkable willingness to adapt and our invaluable singers have risen to the challenges of new production styles and increasingly exacting musical standards in a situation where their average fees are only half of those paid in Europe.

Ann Murray as
Xerxes – Valerie
Masterson as
Romilda
Xerxes Handel/
Minato: *conductor:*
Charles Mackerras,
producer: Nicholas
Hytner, *designer:*
David Fielding,
lighting: Paul Pyant,
translator: Nicholas
Hytner 1985

The most important and, one hopes, sacrosanct of all our traditions is that the company performs in English. It would certainly make a nonsense of all the Baylis ideals about accessibility to address the audience in a foreign language. Indeed, the idea of deliberately addressing anybody, let alone the paying public, in a language they do not understand seems an act of calculated rudeness. Why does anyone do it?

First, to choose a foreign language in the theatre is to signal that this is a dead art-form; that it is more important to exhibit the object authentically, than allow any change which might make it more communicative. If preservation is the priority, then the exhibit must be protected in case it is corroded by the hot breath of the onlooker: a glass panel or protective wrapping is necessary.

Secondly, it is a signal that the public are not participants but visitors. A visitor will look, and admire, but is not necessarily required to contribute anything, other than money. A visitor will need to be kept informed about the exhibit to be admired: most good museums now have portable tape-recorders to tell us what we are looking at, and some opera houses use flashing screens for the same purpose. The result may be beautiful, exquisitely managed, rapturously received, but it is an exhibition, not a theatre. As a matter of basic principle, we assert that in the theatre we address the audience in a language they understand.

In the case of opera, that is emphasized by the relationship between text and music. Music is an abstract medium. It is principally made up of rhythm, pitch, melody and harmony. Language also has rhythm, and can imply melody and pitch, but the one element it has which music does not already possess is *sense*. It is therefore *sense* which the composer seeks as the primary motive in adding words to music. Why do people deny the composer and audience this element of sense? What are the arguments against translation? Mostly, they turn out to be based on assumptions of incompetence – incompetent translators, singers, conductors, theatre architects – but incompetence is not a ground on which to give way on a matter of principle.

The main arguments against performing in English are usually these:

Translation involves compromise

This is unquestionably true. We should assume, however, that a competent translation conveys the *sense* accurately, thereby fulfilling the primary function of the text. Indeed, we may go further and say that, in some cases, sense will be more clearly conveyed in a translation than in the original text, particularly so in the case of composers such as Wagner, who have used obscure forms of their own language. Many, not only English speakers, have noticed that Andrew Porter's translation of the *Ring* is easier to understand than the original German.

There is also, however, no doubt that the ancillary aspects of the text – its sound and rhythm – will be compromised, and that this compromise will transfer it-self to the way in which the music can be performed. The degree of compromise will vary according to the original language and the type of text employed.

A formal, rhymed, poetic text is obviously more problematic than a conversational prose text. The additional burden of rhymes puts another strain on the options of the translator, and a poetic text welds less translatable qualities such as beauty more closely to the sense. The Romance languages, and Italian in particular, are worst affected because they most often employ poetic forms, and also suffer most from the linguistic differences which affect their singability. Beauty of tone and length of line are affected by English vowels, diphthongs and consonants. It is therefore true to say that no performance of an Italian opera can be completely authentic if it is given in English. On the other hand, if we follow this notion of authenticity to its logical conclusion, it is also clear that no performance of an Italian opera would be completely authentic without an entire cast of Italian singers, chorus to match and the architecture and audience of an Italian opera house, all of which add so much to the atmosphere of a performance.

This merely goes to point out the dangers of internationalizing culture. It is much more honest to present performances in our country in a way in which the heart of their meaning is most directly communicated to the audience, thereby remaining true to the social and civic functions of the theatre, without in any way denying that in an Italian opera house you may find a more perfectly authentic rendering of the work itself. Our task should be to prepare performances that have their own integrity and honesty, and do not attempt to ape performances elsewhere.

Another consequence of the prevalent view that Romantic Italian operas should be given in the original language is the prejudice that they are insubstantial as dramatic works. Many people, for instance, consider *Il trovatore* to be dramatically invalid precisely because they have not had the experience of following its text through blow by blow. Summarized, the plot seems absurd, but this reflects an unfamiliarity with its theatrical form (Romantic melodrama) rather than deficiencies in the actual text. Beauty of tone and line may be affected by a translation, but these compromises are no justification for denying text its primary purpose: that of conveying sense.

Quite obviously there are other technical problems in the relationship between all the other languages and English, but they are in a diminishing degree in comparison with the Romance languages; because they are less often in a verse form – with the exception of Wagner – their problems and therefore the compromises involved are significantly less. There are in our experience very few insurmountable problems in translating Russian, Czech or German into English and therefore no excuse whatever for the ridiculous spectacles we have been given recently in this country, where entire casts of American and British singers pretend to sing a language of which they have no knowledge, and which is therefore not a language at all but merely a set of syllables learned by rote.

Terry Jenkins as Orpheus and Lillian Watson as Eurydice **Orpheus in the Underworld** Offenbach/Crémieux & Halévy: *conductor:* Mark Elder, *producer:* David Pountney, *designer:* Gerald Scarfe, *lighting:* Nick Chelton, *translators:* Snoo Wilson/David Pountney 1985

Arthur Davies as Faust in the
madhouse
Faust Gounod/Barbier & Carré:
conductors: Jacques Delacôte/Noël
Davies, *producer:* Ian Judge,
designers: John Gunter/Deirdre
Clancy, *lighting:* Stephen Watson,
translator: Edmund Tracey 1985

Rodney Macann as Klingsor and
Anne Evans as Kundry
Parsifal Wagner: *conductor:*
Reginald Goodall, *producer:*
Joachim Herz, *designer:* Wolf
Münzer, *lighting:* Nick Chelton,
translator: Andrew Porter 1986

We can't hear the words anyway

A rigorously serious view would assert that this objection is entirely irrelevant to the argument. The text should be audible in any language. Clear and committed enunciation of the text is a vital part of any singer's performance, and proper balance with the pit equally important whatever the language. The fact that this kind of discipline and artistic integrity is so rarely found on the international scene, where 'tone' and 'volume' have superseded 'sense' and 'balance', is no argument for a similar capitulation here.

Nevertheless, we must all be aware of the philosophical and political damage done to our case by the fact that the Coliseum's very beautiful and admired acoustic is patchy and, though it flatters voices, it muddies text. The elimination of the acoustic variables in this great theatre will remain a very serious issue, especially for the Board and management of ENO in the future. It is one of the most important of the 'incompetence' arguments, and therefore makes no dent in the *principle* of the 'sense' argument, but it has powerful pragmatic consequences. Addressing this problem is one of the major opportunities afforded by ownership of the building. It can now, at last, be dealt with as part of restoring the theatre to its true glory.

Opera texts are silly, and therefore unimportant

Quite a common argument, and a very ignorant one. Not all opera texts are good, of course, but some (by da Ponte and Hofmannsthal in particular) are brilliant and if the work is at all worth performing, the progression of the drama through text must be a vital part of it. Mostly, the perception that opera texts are worthless comes from hearing summaries of the plots (a trick it is equally easy to pull with Dickens's novels) rather than bar by bar acquaintance with their meaning.

We know the story – we don't need to know what they are saying

This is to deny theatre and music the absolutely vital element of 'time' and spontaneity. It is not sufficient in a drama to know that during this scene X says he loves Y, but to discover it at the same moment that X does. Anything else is drama by tableau. Live theatre is important because of the immediacy of its communication. This is part of its social function. I and my neighbour (who may be entirely unknown to me) share a moment of drama together as we both have our emotion stirred by a particular line. Knowledge of the synopsis is a useful aid, not a substitute.

We are all Europeans now –
surely we can speak enough of each other's language?

One does not have to resort to English self-deprecation about our language deficiencies to nail this piece of Euro-chic pseudery. There are of course brilliant linguists in

Graham Clark as Mephistopheles and Alan Opie as Faust with the students from Krakow (1990 revival)
Dr Faust Busoni, version Antony Beaumont: *conductor:* Mark Elder
producer: David Pountney, *designer:* Stefanos Lazaridis, *lighting:* Nick Chelton, *translator:* Edward J. Dent 1986

the world, but only a minuscule proportion of any audience, even in Paris or Amsterdam, who have much more than restaurant usage of a foreign language. This point goes back to the difference between knowing roughly what is going on, and receiving the text exactly. We all think we know the story of *La bohème*. Yet the *Bohème* text is a very fine one, and its detail contains a great many jokes, whose existence adds a vital dash of lemon to the weepy story. Similarly, the exact reasons why in Act Three Rodolfo cannot bear to be with Mimì any more are always worth hearing afresh in any performance.

Always ask any bluffer who claims to know it all already to explain the precise significance of *all* the letters in *The Marriage of Figaro*.

We come for the music; we don't want to hear the words

Kindly leave the theatre. The text is the bridge between music and the drama. Without text, there is no justification for the stage and all its expensive paraphernalia. The very agreeable pursuit of listening to music only should be carried out in the concert hall.

Philip Langridge as Orpheus
The Mask of Orpheus Harrison
Birtwistle/Peter Zinovieff: *conductor:* Elgar
Howarth, *producer:* David Freeman,
designer: Jocelyn Herbert, *lighting:* Andy
Phillips 1986

Helen Kucharek, Lesley Garrett and Elizabeth McCormack as the 'three little maids from school' (1990 revival) – Bonaventura Bottone as Nanki-Poo and Rosemary Joshua as Yum-Yum (1991 revival) **The Mikado** Sullivan/Gilbert: *conductor:* Peter Robinson, *producer:* Jonathan Miller, *designers:* Stefanos Lazaridis/Sue Blane, *lighting:* David Cunningham 1986

Sally Burgess as Carmen
Carmen Bizet/Meilhac & Halévy:
conductor: Mark Elder, *producer:*
David Pountney, *designer:* Maria
Bjørnson, *lighting:* Paul Pyant,
translator: Anthony Burgess 1986

Josephine Barstow as Tosca and
Neil Howlett as Scarpia
Tosca Puccini/Giacosa & Illica:
conductor: Albert Rosen, *producer:*
Jonathan Miller, *designer:* Stefanos
Lazaridis, *lighting:* Nick Chelton,
translator: Edmund Tracey 1987

Janice Cairns as Amelia
Simon Boccanegra Verdi/Piave,
Montanelli & Boito: *conductor:*
Mark Elder, *producer:* David Alden,
designer: David Fielding, *lighting:*
Pat Collins, *translator:* James
Fenton 1987

Warren Ellsworth as Sergei and
Josephine Barstow as Katerina
(1991 revival)
Lady Macbeth of Mtsensk
Shostakovich/Shostakovich &
Preis: *conductor:* Mark Elder,
producer: David Pountney, *designers:*
Stefanos Lazaridis/Alison Nalder,
lighting: Paul Pyant, *translator:*
David Pountney 1987

The angels
Hansel and Gretel
Humperdinck/Wette: *conductor:*
Mark Elder, *producer:* David
Pountney, *designer:* Stefanos
Lazaridis, *lighting:* Chris Ellis,
translator: David Pountney 1987

Michael Sadler
(Tamate) and
Malcolm Rivers
(Kayama)
Pacific Overtures
Stephen Sondheim/
Sondheim (lyrics) &
Weidman (book):
conductor: James
Holmes, *producer:*
Keith Warner,
designers: Ralph
Koltai/Marie-Jeanne
Lecca, *lighting:* Nick
Chelton 1987

Patrick Power as
Almaviva with the
musicians
**The Barber of
Seville** Rossini/
Sterbini: *conductor:*
Mark Elder, *producer:*
Jonathan Miller,
designer: Tanya
McCallin, *lighting:*
Nick Chelton,
translators: Amanda
& Anthony Holden
1987

David Wilson-Johnson as Mr
Redburn with the chorus (1991
revival)
Billy Budd Britten/Crozier:
conductor: David Atherton, *producer:*
Tim Albery, *designers:* Tom Cairns
& Antony McDonald, *lighting:*
David Cunningham 1988

If we sang in foreign languages, we would be able to cast better singers

We have to recognize that ENO does not nor can ever expect to have the resources to be able to cast at an absolutely international level. Even Covent Garden does not have sufficient resources to do this, and to some extent we should be extremely grateful that our language policy protects us from being involved in the international rat-race to acquire the services of the extremely few international singers who could genuinely be described as 'better' than the people whom we regularly employ, even in Italian opera.

This ignores the effect of singing in a foreign language on the rest of the cast and the chorus. It is much more difficult to obtain vital and direct performances from people who are singing in a foreign language, especially those who are not accustomed to doing so. There are very, very few people around the world who are talented enough to divert all the nerve-endings that go to make up an electrifying stage performance through the medium of a language foreign to them. In this context there is clearly no comparison between our emotional empathy with the language of our birth and a learned language. When we consider this factor in relation to the singers of the smaller parts and the chorus, it must be obvious why these areas are so often less vivid, energetic and communicative at Covent Garden than they are at our own house. It is also a well-known phenomenon that singers often appear to much greater advantage at ENO than they do at Covent Garden, partly due to a flattering acoustic, but also due to the enormous infusion of spontaneity and communication afforded by performing in their own language, and interacting with those around them in their own language.

ENO has the reputation of a provincial company because it performs in English

This is a two-edged argument. We do not and would never have the resources to compete on the highest international level. Our reputation as a distinctive house is much more firmly grounded because we sing in English, and because we stand out every year more significantly against the trend towards original-language performances with surtitles. We are a *national* house, as our name states. This is also one of our strongest political cards for the maintenance of two houses in London.

Why then can we not maintain our distinctive policy but do occasional performances in the original language?

If we have established as a matter of principle that our policy is the correct one, it seems very weak-minded to compromise on it. It is merely giving ammunition to those who would like to shoot down the entire policy, and with it probably the existence of two opera companies in London. A two-tier approach would also cause great problems for the management. It is well-known that many singers and conductors take the prejudiced view that performing in the original language is superior, not least because of the added workload of learning translations. It would be very difficult to prevent some singers who do have international careers from insisting that if they were to sing in the house, it would have to be in one of our original-language productions. The control of this policy would very rapidly fall out of the management's hands and an extremely unpleasant A and B system would arise. Furthermore, it would have a damaging effect on costs. As we maintain our individual policy, people do understand that they should not expect fees here to be the same as they are at Covent Garden (they are, in fact, on average half). If they were coming here to sing in Italian, it would be much more difficult to sustain this.

Surtitles (*aka* theatrical condoms – a piece of celluloid interposed between the audience and the performers)

Let us admit at once that audiences like them. The same is apparently true of hanging. Neither would get our vote. There are, after all, limits to democracy. Everyone (or at least the arty crowd) has become accustomed to subtitles at the movies . . . but then we don't have to avert our eyes from the action to read on, and film is a mechanical, 'frozen' medium anyway.

But why *not* have surtitles? Why not, for instance, contradict the efforts of the theatre architects who have spent centuries perfecting designs which concentrate the audience's attention on the stage, by installing little flashing screens in a part of the proscenium that was specifically designed only to be looked at during the interval? This splendid idea ruins the performance as well as the design of the building when the lights are up. Bravo!

Why not contradict the efforts of the composers and dramatists who have striven to integrate music, text and action into one concentrated thread by isolating a single element miles above most of the audience's heads?

Why not render useless the priceless comic timing of our singers by making the audience laugh at the crib sheet instead?

Why not have surtitles also describing the nature of the music? 'This bit is in F major.' 'This is the cup and saucer motif.' 'This is an inversion of Wozzeck's madness motif.'

Why leave it at the text? Why not flash up instructions about emotional involvement? 'Start crying now' – 'Isn't Pinkerton a cad?' Why not explain the production (at last)? 'Cornfield – a symbol of nature at the mercy of capitalist exploitation.' Why not give really useful information? 'England 243 for 7', 'Clamping lorry in St Martin's Lane' or 'Only 20 minutes until *Nessun dorma*.'

In fact, surtitles do strike directly at the integrity of what we do because they are an extraneous technical device superimposed on a delicately poised balance of interaction and participation between audience and performer. Once we have given in to this 'quick fix' solution, the inevitable long-term deterioration of artistic

Benjamin Luxon as Papageno with Daniel Ison, Simon Millington and Daniel Meiland as the Three Boys (1990 revival)
The Magic Flute
Mozart/Schikaneder: *conductor:* Ivan Fischer, *producer:* Nicholas Hytner, *designer:* Bob Crowley, *lighting:* Nick Chelton, *translator:* Jeremy Sams 1988

44

The entertainment at Flora's party
La traviata Verdi/Piave: *conductor:*
Mark Elder, *producer:* David
Pountney, *designer:* Stefanos
Lazaridis, *lighting:* Chris Ellis,
translator: David Pountney 1988

John Connell as Chub, Marian
Martin as the Woman with an
Ordinary Nose and Shelagh
Squires as the Woman with a
Purple Nose (1991 revival)
Christmas Eve Rimsky-Korsakov:
conductor: Albert Rosen, *producer:*
David Pountney, *designer:* Sue
Blane, *lighting:* Chris Ellis,
translator: David Pountney 1988

integrity on all sides may be summed up as 'why bother?' Why should the singer bother to acquire the discipline of good diction, why should the conductor bother to restrain and control the orchestra for the sake of balance, why should the audience bother to concentrate on listening, why should the Board bother with improving the acoustics of our theatre, why should designers bother to consider, amidst all the other restrictions, that an acoustic surround is an important consideration? Above all, why bother to sing in English at all?

The second and more profound consequence of surtitles is to affect the integrity of the type of performance we offer. Theatre is meant to be a forum for active participation by the audience. We do not invite our audience to be detached connoisseurs, taking part in a 'tasting', but to roll up their sleeves for a family meal. But participation demands that the sense arrives like a glowing hot coal, straight from the mouth of the singer, and strikes instantly at the heads and hearts of the audience. The surtitle is a catastrophic gooseberry in this vital act of theatrical intercourse. It is a device for the tourist, who looks but does not participate, and this is a betrayal of theatre's civic function as a place of communal experience. Tourists are welcome to observe, but once they take over, the event they come to watch has been destroyed. The journey through an experience led by the performers cannot achieve its true emotional impact if it is to be punctuated by frequent reference to a flashing Baedeker.

Brecht, one of the most acute analysts of the theatrical experience, hated opera precisely because of its emotionally-involving nature. In trying to evolve his theory of 'alienation' it is no accident that one of the things he advocated was 'textual theatre' which involved the use of ideological or philosophical 'surtitles'. These, he argued, would detach the audience from performance, and encourage in them an attitude of aloof, sceptical, critical judgement. He was right. This is the subliminal consequence of referring to 'dry' or 'cold' text (as opposed to the hot, wet text from the singers' lips) during the performance, and there is no more insidious way to destroy the ultimate integrity and value of an operatic performance.

Is it naïve to place such a high value on 'integrity'? Will the cynical process of political decisions about the future of our company really be affected by such an invisible factor? We think they will. Artistic integrity is an essential ingredient in the philosophical justification for subsidy. And a second opera house in a declining economy must always be vulnerable to reductive schemes for rationalization. It is precisely the integrity and individuality of ENO, and the fact that it has kept faith with a very great tradition, that is its strongest guarantee for an independent future. Surtitles for ENO would be irresponsible both to the integrity of the art-form, and to the company itself.

Rosa Mannion as Cordelia and Monte Jaffe as Lear
Lear Aribert Reimann/Claus H. Henneberg: *conductor:* Paul Daniel, *producer:* Eike Gramss, *designers:* Eberhard Matthies & Renate Schmitzer, *lighting:* Paul Pyant, *translator:* Desmond Clayton 1989

One tradition that the company has fought hard to rebuild, with only patchy success, is the tradition of the composer in the opera house. It goes without saying that no serious opera company can simply go on churning out works from the past without reflecting on the future of the medium itself, but how contemporary composers are reconnected both with the theatre and with the audience is far from obvious. One first step was to re-establish the idea that new work in the opera house was as normal as it is in the theatre, hence the plans to present a new work automatically each season. To protect these fragile plants against cold financial winds, they were placed cunningly at the start of the financial year when miraculous and wholly unfounded optimism must be the rule. They were also carefully restricted in their scale. The result is that the series has survived despite its horrific comparative cost (the financial gain of replacing a new commission by a revival of *Bohème* does not bear thinking about), with the important psychological message to composers that writing opera is not a forlorn pursuit with no prospect of performance. But it cannot be counted a great success from the audience's point of view partly because, at this early stage of rebuilding bridges between audience and composer, it remains, like much modern art, an exercise for professionals rather than the audience.

Of course, the dislocation between audience and art-form in our century is not confined to music. It is equally the case in most art-forms except *the* twentieth-century form, the cinema. But a *theatre* without an audience is a very lonely place. We attempted to counteract this dislocation with our twentieth-century season, but we did not really get back from the audience the answers we wanted. Almost everyone in the music profession reveres *Wozzeck* and *Pelléas* as outstanding operas, yet by the stern judgement that Verdi would have applied – looking at the box office returns – these works remain more for the professionals or at least devotees than for the general public. Indeed, for the purposes of example, the universally revered case of Alban Berg has turned out to be opera's blindest alley. Few composers who entered it have come out with a success.

Benjamin Luxon as Falstaff
Falstaff Verdi/ Boito: *conductor:* Mark Elder, *producer:* David Pountney, *designer:* Marie-Jeanne Lecca, *lighting:* Paul Pyant, *translator:* Amanda Holden 1989

Jonathan Summers as Onegin
Eugene Onegin Tchaikovsky/
Shilovsky & Tchaikovsky:
conductor: Mark Elder, *producer:*
Graham Vick, *designer:* Sally
Jacobs, *lighting:* Nick Chelton,
translator: David Lloyd-Jones 1989

Richard Taylor as
Gustavus (1991
revival)
A Masked Ball
Verdi/Somma:
conductor: Mark
Elder, *producer:*
David Alden,
designer: David
Fielding, *lighting:*
Wolfgang Göbbel
(revived by Paul
Taylor), *translator:*
Edmund Tracey
1989

Christopher Robson as Akhnaten and Marie Angel as Tye **Akhnaten** Philip Glass/Philip Glass, Shalom Goldman, Robert Israel & Richard Riddell: *conductor:* Paul Daniel, *producer:* David Freeman, *designer:* David Roger, *lighting:* Richard Riddell, 1985 (photo: Jim Caldwell)

Indeed, composers in general show little sign of giving a damn for the audience. This, we might say, is the downside of subsidy and it is a pity because the potential audience, even for a meagre five performances, is still 12,000 people. This is not a number that can be made up by a coterie. What is worse is that so-called 'serious' composers do not much respect the theatre either. Musical culture generally rests on the belief that the composer is right. But in the theatre, the modern composer is generally wrong and for good reasons. They have few role models: since Puccini and Strauss, only Britten and Henze have enjoyed any kind of real success in the theatre and, in Britain, the tragedy of Tippett squandering his prodigious talent on material that has so little *theatrical* viability instead of acting as a dire warning has merely set a bad example. And yet we live in a country of out-standingly fertile, inventive and successful playwrights. This is mad. But it is not half as maddening as the fact that in all the many discussions we have instigated between writers and composers, the composers have very rarely shown any sign of acknowledging that they were, theatrically, a very unsuccessful breed who desperately needed the help and experience of their collaborators to re-establish a tradition of new music in the theatre.

After our symposium on the creation of the Contemporary Opera Studio at Dartington, many of the 30 or so writers who took part were astounded by the

The pastoral: Peter Coleman-Wright as Colin and Ann Howard as Mrs Worthing (Astraea) **The Plumber's Gift** David Blake/John Birtwhistle: *conductor:* Lionel Friend, *producer:* Richard Jones, *designer:* Nigel Lowery, *lighting:* Pat Collins 1989

Catherine Zeta Jones as Mae and
Philip Gould as Dick
Street Scene Kurt Weill/Langston
Hughes (lyrics) & Elmer Rice
(book): *conductors:* Carl Davis/
James Holmes, *producer:* David
Pountney, *designer:* David Fielding,
lighting: Paul Pyant, *choreographer:*
David Toguri 1989

Laurence Dale as Telemachus and
Sally Burgess as Minerva
The Return of Ulysses
Monteverdi/Badoaro: *conductor:*
Paul Daniel, *producer:* David
Freeman, *designer:* David Roger,
floor: Anya Gallaccio, *lighting:*
Richard Riddell, *translator:* Anne
Ridler 1989

Ann Murray as Beatrice
Beatrice and Benedict Berlioz: *conductor:* Mark Elder, *producer:* Tim Albery,
designers: Tom Cairns & Antony McDonald, *lighting:* Wolfgang Göbbel,
translators: Amanda Holden & Marty Cruickshank 1989

Richard Angas as
the Cook and
Bonaventura
Bottone as
Truffaldino
**The Love for
Three Oranges**
Prokofiev: *conductor:*
David Atherton,
producer: Richard
Jones, *designers:* The
Brothers Quay &
Sue Blane, *lighting:*
Nick Chelton,
translator: David
Lloyd-Jones 1989

insularity of the established composers there. The self-perpetuating academic coterie
of music critics, equally uneasy about their credentials in the theatre, actually per-
petuate this insularity and insidiously create a division between 'serious' composers
producing heavily subsidized art objects for professionals, and those frivolous and
trivial people who work in a more widely communicative style. This false division is
partly responsible for the fact that the history of post-Britten opera is a void only
occasionally illuminated by immensely worthy failures. This is the divisive aesthetic
which condemns Kurt Weill because he 'sold out' to the commercial theatre. It was
important to us, at ENO, to mount *Street Scene* precisely because it is such a startling
example of a composer who set out to learn the language of his audience. It is no
accident that the compassion for other human beings that that implies is also the
overriding quality of this work. Another much sneered-at figure is Philip Glass,
whose critics rarely show any signs of picking up the challenge he offers: 'Don't crit-
icize, do better!' No one would suggest that minimalism is going to play a major
part in the long-term future of opera, but it was a very necessary phenomenon – a

Jonathan Summers
as Macbeth
Macbeth Verdi/
Piave after
Shakespeare:
conductor: Mark
Elder, *producer:*
David Pountney,
designer: Stefanos
Lazaridis, *lighting:*
Paul Pyant,
translator: Jeremy
Sams 1990

desperately needed antidote to the plague of notes and complexity. The one person who had the balance right between the popular and the serious was brutally silenced, in the theatre, by Stalin. Now that it is receiving more and more productions, Shostakovich's *Lady Macbeth of Mtsensk* is emerging as the most popular post-*verismo* work of our century. What would have happened if we had ten of these?

Nonetheless, there is hope – quite tremendous hope, in fact. The new commission series has established new opera as a financial habit at ENO and has begun to enable the company to relearn its commissioning role: the blame for failure belongs to us, too. The younger generation of composers, liberated from modernism, is much more open to wider influences from the theatre, television and other musical cultures. At ENO's Contemporary Opera Studio we see among composers a much greater readiness to embrace the theatre and all its potential. In the 90s Judith Weir, Mark-Anthony Turnage, Benedict Mason, Julian Grant, Jonathan Dove and no doubt many others have an opportunity to rebuild a tradition of new writing in which the audience participate out of pleasure rather than duty.

And in the most explicit tribute to Lilian Baylis that the company has made, there is hope that a growing body of young people, nurtured by the tireless invention and creativity of the Baylis Programme – our outreach department – will come forward to enrich operatic life on both sides of the footlights in the next century. The company now has the enormous psychological buzz of owning its own theatre and this raises great prospects for it to be developed into the kind of friendly, accessible and popular home for culture that Lilian Baylis would have loved. It has an exciting and innovative new team at its head. We wish them well, and to remember that, when God says 'No', it is not the end of the world.

Peter Jonas
Mark Elder
David Pountney

The family at the death-bed of
Buoso Donati: George Mosley,
Dennis Wicks, Terry Jenkins,
Marie Slorach, Anne Collins,
Shelagh Squires, Michael Druiett,
David Maxwell Anderson
Gianni Schicchi Puccini/Forzano:
conductor: Charles Mackerras,
producer: Stephen Unwin, *designer:*
Ultz, *lighting:* Richard Riddell,
translator: Edward Downes 1990

Vivian Tierney as Clarissa
Clarissa Robin Holloway/
Holloway after Richardson:
conductor: Oliver Knussen, *producer:*
David Pountney, *designer:* David
Fielding, *lighting:* Paul Pyant,
choreographer: Ian Spink 1990

Gwynne Howell as Bluebeard and
Sally Burgess as Judith
Bluebeard's Castle Bartók/
Balázs: *conductor:* Mark Elder,
producer: David Alden, *designer:*
Nigel Lowery, *lighting:* Richard
Riddell, *translator:* John Lloyd
Davies 1991

Jean Rigby as Jocasta and the
chorus
Oedipus Rex Stravinsky/
Cocteau: *conductor:* Mark Elder,
producer: David Alden, *designer:*
Nigel Lowery, *lighting:* Richard
Riddell 1991

Donald Maxwell as Wozzeck
Wozzeck Berg/Berg after Büchner: *conductor:* Mark Elder, *producer:* David Pountney, *designer:* Stefanos Lazaridis, *lighting:* David Cunningham, *translators:* Eric Blackall & Vida Harford 1990

Cathryn Pope as Mélisande and Thomas Randle as Pelléas
Pelléas and Mélisande Debussy/Maeterlinck: *conductor:* Mark Elder, *producer:* David Pountney, *designer:* Marie-Jeane Lecca, *lighting:* Richard Riddell, *translator:* Hugh Macdonald 1990

Craig Liddiard as the Apprentice
and Philip Langridge as Grimes –
The Borough
Peter Grimes Britten/Slater:
conductor: David Atherton, *producer:*
Tim Albery, *designer:* Hildegard
Bechtler, *lighting:* Jean Kalman
1991

English National Opera – A Brief History

It is difficult to fix the birthdate of the company which is now English National Opera. In 1898, the pioneering charity worker Emma Cons summoned her 23-year-old niece, Lilian Baylis, to help among the destitutes of Waterloo. She ascribed many of the evils of moral and social depravity to the 'demon drink', and thought that teetotal entertainment would be a useful distraction. So Lilian Baylis started a series of costumed opera recitals at the Old Vic theatre. Convinced that the best of culture should be available to all, in 1912 Lilian Baylis obtained a licence for staged performances and started giving cut-down versions of opera alternating with Shakespeare. Performances continued throughout the First World War, attracting an enthusiastic public from all over the capital, and afterwards the Old Vic's prestige drew actors and singers who were prepared to work for minimal pay. It was then the only permanent company in the capital devoted to the classics.

The first music directors of the opera company were Charles Corri and Lawrance Collingwood, who shared a talent for orchestration for the semi-professional band of eighteen players: in 1920 Corri achieved an ambition by arranging *Tristan and Isolde*. In the same year, Clive Carey produced *The Marriage of Figaro* in a translation by his friend and mentor, the Cambridge musicologist Edward Dent, and proved the value of more rehearsals and better translations. They added *The Magic Flute* (then still a rarity) and *Don Giovanni* to the repertory. Although Lilian Baylis was omnipresent at the Old Vic, notoriously concerning herself with every aspect of its work, she allowed her staff and performers considerable freedom. Continually hard-pressed for finance, she spent little or nothing on costumes and sets and she was, in the words of her biographer, 'deeply suspicious of spectacle, showmanship and glamour'. She used to harangue the audiences, famous for their noisy participation, about the importance of supporting all the productions. Her vision of a people's theatre remained undimmed and in 1928 she even agreed with Ninette de Valois to take on a small group of dancers.

By 1925 Lilian Baylis realized that one theatre was not big enough for both theatre and opera companies and she determined to open an 'Old Vic' at Sadler's Wells in Islington, where a historic theatrical site had gone to ruin. It took six years of fundraising for Sadler's Wells to be rebuilt, and it opened (with a deficit on the building project of £20,000) on 6 January 1931, with Shakespeare, and a week later the opera company performed *Carmen*. Overnight the number of performances of Miss Baylis's companies was doubled and, for a few years, opera alternated with spoken theatre in both theatres; in 1934/35 the Opera Company was established in Islington, where it remained (apart from an interlude of wartime touring) until 1968.

At Sadler's Wells the musical standards improved enormously with a professional chorus and, eventually, a permanent orchestra. Collingwood introduced several important Russian operas and his successor Warwick Braithwaite, as well as the producers (Sumner Austin, Clive Carey, J. B. Gordon, colloquially known as the

'Soviet'), broadened the repertory still further. There were new British operas by Holst, Stanford, Vaughan Williams, Arthur Benjamin and Ethel Smyth. By 1937 more than fifty operas had been given. In the eight-month season there were performances almost every night – Lilian Baylis preferred a varied programme to long runs, and she did her best to oppose revivals of any novelties which had not immediately proved popular. She had to rely on philanthropy for much financial support and she succeeded in impressing her personal style of management on what quickly became two companies (opera and ballet) based at the new theatre. The ballet, under Constant Lambert, attracted brilliant talents such as Robert Helpmann and Margot Fonteyn. 'Her supreme gift was getting other people to perform miracles for her', wrote Hugh Walpole, who also acclaimed the 1936 production of *The Mastersingers of Nuremberg* with the cry: 'We HAVE a national opera!' There were guest visits from Beecham and Barbirolli, and singers such as Maggie Teyte, Florence Austral, Astra Desmond and Miriam Licette, but the nucleus comprised artists of the calibre of Joan Cross, Molly De Gunst, Edith Coates, Henry Wendon, Redvers Llewellyn, John Hargreaves, Roderick Lloyd and Ronald Stear. The spirit of enterprise which animated this team remained in many memories as a golden age.

The state of the company at Lilian Baylis's death in 1937 may be judged from the calibre of new productions: under the leadership of Tyrone Guthrie *The Valkyrie* was given in December, and *Der Rosenkavalier* in March 1939. During the war the theatre was requisitioned and in 1940 Guthrie moved the centre of operations to Burnley. Joan Cross became the manager of a touring troupe of twenty, raising war-time spirits and gathering a huge popularity. By 1942 (when the composer Benjamin Britten and tenor Peter Pears returned to England from America), they were regularly playing in the West End: at the New Theatre (now the Albery) in St Martin's Lane with *Così fan tutte* and *The Bartered Bride*. Already in 1944 opinions were being aired about the future of opera in Britain and Edward Dent vigorously campaigned for the Wells, realizing that post-war governments would have other priorities than the arts. It was a blow that Covent Garden was reconstituted as a company to perform in English with a grant of £25,000 a year, and the Wells was promised only £10,000 – and that without the financial support of the ballet, which was to be renamed the Royal Ballet and housed at the Royal Opera House.

Nevertheless, in 1945 Britten's new opera *Peter Grimes* re-opened Sadler's Wells. It marked more than the return home; with this opera the company made history, introducing a major figure to international opera, the first English composer since Purcell to be so. At this very unsettled time, the chorus and orchestra took some convincing (and Britten never wrote for the company again) but the audiences recognized a masterpiece. Pears remembered: 'They felt that the tensions played out and to some extent reconciled on stage were connected with their lives, and that Britten could set the English language in a way that didn't ring false.'

A period of consolidation followed, establishing the Sadler's Wells policies: accessibility in seat prices, good translations and a preference for a team per-

Cathryn Pope as Susanna and Christine Botes as Cherubino
Figaro's Wedding
Mozart/da Ponte: *conductor:* Paul Daniel, *producer:* Graham Vick, *designer:* Richard Hudson, *lighting:* Nick Chelton, *translator:* Jeremy Sams 1991

formance instead of a star system. Tyrone Guthrie produced *Falstaff*, *Carmen* and *The Barber of Seville*; following Verdi's *Simon Boccanegra* (1948) there was *Don Carlos* in 1951, the year of the first Janáček opera to be staged in Britain, *Katya Kabanova*. For sixteen years from 1952 the brilliant manager and pianist Norman Tucker directed the fortunes of the company with a succession of Music Directors, including Alexander Gibson and Colin Davis. The connection with the theatre traditions of the Old Vic was maintained through productions by George Devine, Michel Saint-Denis and Glen Byam Shaw, and the latter became permanently attached to the Company after he retired from the directorship of the Royal Shakespeare Company at the end of the 50s. Sadler's Wells attracted many Commonwealth artists of international stature who swelled the ensemble until, by 1960, there were 33 principals and 18 guest artists. In particular, the Australian Charles Mackerras is associated with Janáček and Mozart, while Rossini operas emerged after decades of neglect – even a century in the case of *The Thieving Magpie* – thanks to the genial skill of Tom Hammond. There were important rare Verdi productions such as *Ernani*, *Attila* and *A Masked Ball*. The company toured Britain incessantly, with one group in London and the other in the regions, and there were European tours to festivals on both sides of the Iron Curtain, as well as a tour in 1960 to Australia.

The decision to move to the London Coliseum in 1968 was prompted by the long-delayed and last-minute rejection by the Government of a proposal to build a National Opera House on the South Bank, next to the National Theatre where the Old Vic company was now housed. Coincidentally, a production by Glen Byam Shaw and John Blatchley of *The Mastersingers* (the first since that famous one in 1936) had brought both choruses of the company together under the baton of Reginald Goodall, with a first-rate cast. This proved that the musical standard had never been higher, and gave confidence to the Managing Director, Stephen Arlen, to take a lease on the London Coliseum, the largest theatre in the West End (with 2,358 seats). This historic location, built in 1904 as a 'theatre of varieties', was a vast challenge for the company, and the transfer of *The Mastersingers* triumphantly sealed the success of this new era. After prolonged negotiations, the company name was officially changed in 1974 to English National Opera – thereby recognizing what had been unofficially the case since 1931.

The 70s were years of renewing the repertory in the grand space of the new theatre and were especially associated with Wagner. In 1972 the success of *The Valkyrie* with Rita Hunter, Norman Bailey and Alberto Remedios, and Goodall's conducting, marked the birth of a *Ring* cycle in English. These performances, which were repeated in many theatres on tour in England, developed into one of the great achievements of post-war opera, ideally synthesizing the company aims of all-round achievement in drama and design as well as music. ENO has played a crucial role in nurturing the singers who are now the stars of Bayreuth: Graham Clark, Anne Evans, Linda Finnie and John Tomlinson.

Lord Harewood became Managing Director after Arlen's untimely death in 1972 and steered an adventurous course with Mackerras as Music Director, later

Monte Jaffe as Timon
Timon of Athens Oliver, after
Shakespeare: *conductor:* Graeme
Jenkins, *producer:* Graham Vick,
designer: Chris Dyer, *lighting:* Chris
Jaeger 1991

Lesley Garrett as Adele and
Andrew Shore as Colonel Frank
Die Fledermaus J. Strauss/
Haffner & Genée: *conductor:* Adam
Fischer, *producer:* Richard Jones,
designer: Nigel Lowery, *lighting:* Pat
Collins, *translators:* Leonard
Hancock & David Pountney 1991

Holiday mood in Hellabrunn; far
left: Hilary Summers and Maria
Moll as the Stablegirl and
Innkeeper's daughter; far right:
Joseph Evans as the Prince and
Richard Angas as the Innkeeper
Königskinder Humperdinck/
Rosmer: *conductor:* Mark Elder,
producer: David Pountney, *designer:*
Sue Blane, *lighting:* Paul Pyant,
translator: David Pountney 1991

Edmund Barham as Carlos and Jonathan Summers as Posa **Don Carlos** Verdi/ Méry & du Locle: *conductor:* Mark Elder, *producer:* David Pountney, *designer:* David Fielding, *lighting:* Paul Pyant, *translator:* Andrew Porter 1992

Thomas Randle as Dionysus **The Bacchae/ BAKXAI** John Buller after Euripides: *conductor:* Martin André, *producer:* Julia Hollander, *designers:* Hildegard Bechtler & Nicky Gillibrand, *lighting:* Alan Burrett 1992

joined by Colin Graham as Director of Productions. They, together with the translator and artistic adviser Edmund Tracey, paid attention to British premières but also introduced some of the most challenging works of the operatic orchestral repertory: Strauss's *Rosenkavalier*, *Salome* and *Arabella*, Debussy's *Pelléas and Mélisande*, as well as a staging of Berlioz's *The Damnation of Faust*. Many of these works, as well as the continuation of the Janáček tradition, were a hallmark of the Coliseum sound and a new generation of interpreters has emerged ready to tackle the larger acoustic of the theatre, and to take the standards of ENO performance with them when they appear on other stages. Also during Lord Harewood's seasons there were spectacular productions by John Copley and Colin Graham of the main repertory pieces, which set new standards of staging and design, further developed by guest producers such as Joachim Herz, Harry Kupfer, Jean-Claude Auvray and, above all, Jonathan Miller, with his *'ancien-régime' Marriage of Figaro* and 'Little Italy' *Rigoletto*. This era reached a climax in 1984, when ENO became the first major British opera company to make an extended tour of the USA with the North American première of *Gloriana*, and highly successful performances of Prokofiev's *War and Peace*.

Mark Elder became Music Director in 1979, succeeding Sir Charles Groves. During his years the musical standards have won many awards, including the Royal Philharmonic Society's Award to the orchestra as the best orchestral ensemble in Britain in 1990. David Pountney succeeded Colin Graham as Director of Productions in 1982 and his own productions of a broad repertory ranging from Czech composers to Verdi, and from Offenbach to Shostakovich have caught the imagination of the public. In 1985 Peter Jonas took over as General Director and brought the company increasingly to the forefront of public debate about opera in Britain, although the company is no longer obliged by the government to tour. In 1990, however, ENO became the first major foreign opera company to undertake a full-scale tour of the then Soviet Union (Kiev, Moscow and Leningrad), confirming ENO's role as a national cultural ambassador. In 1992 the Coliseum freehold was purchased with government support, so that the company's future was assured.

While there has been no new *Ring*, there have been many large-scale company achievements. Berg's *Wozzeck*, Debussy's *Pelléas and Mélisande* and Shostakovich's *Lady Macbeth of Mtsensk* featured at the heart of the 1990/91 season which was dedicated to operas of our century – mixed with Mozart to mark the 200th anniversary of the death of this composer. At the same time it is possible to contrast these large undertakings with the success of operas involving small orchestral forces, such as Monteverdi's *Orfeo* and *Return of Ulysses*, or Britten's *Rape of Lucretia* and *Turn of the Screw*. Fixing ENO at the 'heart of British operatic life' has been an ambition of these years with the annual performance of a commissioned opera, and the continual encouragement of new conductors, singers, producers, designers and choreographers.

Nicholas John

Set design by James Merifield
Princess Ida
Gilbert and Sullivan: *conductor:* Jane Glover, *producer:* Ken Russell 1992

Set design by Richard Hudson
The Force of Destiny Verdi/Piave & Ghislanzoni: *conductor:* Mark Elder, *producer:* Nicholas Hytner, *translator:* Jeremy Sams 1992

The Judgement of Solomon: Keel Watson as King Solomon,
with the children of six inner-London primary schools
The Queen of Sheba's Legs Julian Grant/Marina Warner: *conductor:* Alec Roth, *producer:* Lynn Schey,
designer: David Blight, *lighting:* Marian Staal/Christine Walton
The Baylis Programme at St Martin in the Fields, 1991